CLASS SCHEDUL

Name _____ School _____ Grade _____

MONDAY	Time	Subject	Room

TUESDAY	Time	Subject	Room

WEDNESDAY	Time	Subject	Room

THURSDAY	Time	Subject	Room

FRIDAY	Time	Subject	Room

Made in the USA
Monee, IL
22 December 2021

86886507R00090